Blogging for Educators: Writing for Professional Le
By Starr Sackstein @mssackstein

Principal Professional Development: Leading Learning in the Digital Age
By Joseph Sanfelippo @Joesanfelippofc and Tony Sinanis @TonySinanis

The Power of Branding: Telling Your School's Story
By Tony Sinanis @TonySinanis and Joseph Sanfelippo @Joesanfelippofc

The Relevant Educator: How Connectedness Empowers Learning
By Tom Whitby @tomwhitby and Steven W. Anderson @web20classroom

Worlds of Making

*Best Practices for Establishing a
Makerspace for Your School*

Laura Fleming

CORWIN
A SAGE Company

CORWIN
A SAGE Company

FOR INFORMATION:

Corwin
A SAGE Company
2455 Teller Road
Thousand Oaks, California 91320
(800) 233-9936
www.corwin.com

SAGE Publications Ltd.
1 Oliver's Yard
55 City Road
London EC1Y 1SP
United Kingdom

SAGE Publications India Pvt. Ltd.
B 1/I 1 Mohan Cooperative Industrial Area
Mathura Road, New Delhi 110 044
India

SAGE Publications Asia-Pacific Pte. Ltd.
3 Church Street
#10-04 Samsung Hub
Singapore 049483

Printed in the United States of America

A catalog record of this book is available from the Library of Congress.

ISBN 978-1-4833-8282-1

This book is printed on acid-free paper.

Executive Editor: Arnis Burvikovs
Associate Editor: Ariel Price
Editorial Assistant: Andrew Olson
Production Editor: Amy Schroller
Copy Editor: Tammy Giesmann
Typesetter: C&M Digitals (P) Ltd.
Proofreader: Liann Lech
Cover and Interior Designer: Janet Kiesel
Marketing Manager: Lisa Lysne

Certified Chain of Custody
Promoting Sustainable Forestry
www.sfiprogram.org
SFI-01268

SUSTAINABLE FORESTRY INITIATIVE

SFI label applies to text stock

15 16 17 18 19 10 9 8 7 6 5 4 3 2

Contents

Preface

W elcome to the Corwin Connected Educators Series.

Last year, Ariel Price, Arnis Burvikovs, and I assembled a great list of authors for the Fall 2014 books in the Corwin Connected Educators Series. As leaders in their field of connected education, they all provided practical, short books that helped educators around the world find new ways to connect. The books in the Spring 2015 season will be equally as beneficial for educators.

We have all seen momentous changes for educators. States debate the use of the Common Core State Standards, and teachers and leaders still question the use of technology, while some of their students have to disconnect and leave it at home because educators do not know how to control learning on devices. Many of the Series authors worked in schools where they were sometimes the only ones trying to encourage use of technology tools at the same time their colleagues tried to ban it. Through their PLNs they were able to find others who were trying to push the envelope.

This spring, we have a list of authors who are known for pushing the envelope. Some are people who wrote books for the Fall 2014 season, while others are brand new to the series. What they have in common is that they see a different type of school for students, and they write about ideas that all schools should be practicing now.

Rafranz Davis discusses *The Missing Voices in EdTech*. She looks at and discusses how we need to bring more diverse voices to the connected world because those voices will enrich how we learn and the way we think. Starr Sackstein, a teacher in New York City, writes about blogging for reflection in her book *Blogging for Educators*. Twitter powerhouse Steven W. Anderson returns to the Series to bring us *Content Curation*, as do the very engaging Joseph M. Sanfelippo and Tony Sinanis with their new book, *Principal Professional Development*. Mark Barnes rounds out the comeback authors with his book on *5 Skills for the Global Learner*. Thomas C. Murray and Jeffrey Zoul bring a very practical "how to" for teachers and leaders in their book *Leading Professional Learning*, and Makerspaces extraordinaire Laura Fleming brings her expertise with *Worlds of Making*.

I am insanely excited about this book series. As a former principal I know time is in short supply, and teachers and leaders need something they can read today and put into practice tomorrow. That is the exciting piece about technology; it can help enhance your practices by providing you with new ideas and helping you connect with educators around the world.

The books can be read in any order, and each will provide information on the tools that will keep us current in the digital age. We also look forward to continuing the series with more books from experts on connectedness.

As Michael Fullan has been saying for many years, technology is not the right driver, good pedagogy is, and the books in this connected series focus on practices that will lead to good pedagogy in our digital age. To assist readers in their connected experience, we have created the Corwin Connected Educators companion website where readers can connect with the authors and find resources to help further their experience. The website can be found at www.corwin.com/connectededucators. It is our hope that we can meet you where you are in your digital journey, and bring you up to the next level.

Peter M. DeWitt, EdD
@PeterMDeWitt

About the Author

 **Laura Fleming** has been an educator in the state of New Jersey for 17 years. She has been both a classroom teacher and media specialist in Grades K–8 and currently is a Library Media Specialist for Grades 9–12. Laura is a strong advocate of using New Media and Vanguard Techniques for Interactive and Transmedia (multi-platform) Storytelling. She has played a prominent role in education as a writer and speaker and has served as an educational consultant on next-generation teaching methods and tools. Laura has also consulted on Transmedia properties, working with producers to help maximize the value of their creations and toolsets for teachers and students.

Laura's goal is to create learning experiences that empower and equip students with necessary skills to effectively produce and consume content across multiple media platforms. She is also driven to enable educators and cohorts in applying these innovative methods and cutting-edge technology in their fields of expertise.

Recently, Laura created a digital badge-based professional development platform which can be found at www.worlds-of-learning-nmhs.com. Her library Makerspace has garnered national attention and has served as an inspiration for schools across the country. She is also a recipient of the National School Boards "20 to Watch" in Educational Technology Leadership for 2014.

Introduction

Since launching my makerspace, I have received, almost on a daily basis, inquiries from educators nationally who wanted to create their own makerspace. Their questions ranged from budgets to purchases to setup and facilitation. Many of their questions will be answered in this book, along with drawing attention to the Maker Movement in general and the profound impact it is having on education. Special focus will be on the library makerspace since that is where we see a lot of this taking place as a way to keep libraries relevant and vibrant. Educators will also learn how to make the most of their makerspace by leveraging the resources they have available to them to create their own robust unique learning environment.

Worlds of Making will focus on the nuts and bolts of imagining, planning, creating, and managing your own makerspace. This book will answer many of the questions that you and your colleagues may have about the processes involved in establishing a makerspace, ranging from consultation (of colleagues and students) to formulating your ideas, from agreeing budgets to making purchases, and from setup to facilitation and operation. In this short introduction, we begin by examining the Maker Movement in general, and we take a look at the profound impact it is having on education, an impact that has really made itself felt only in the last two or three years, even though the concept of the makerspace has been around for quite some time. We will have a special focus on the library makerspace, since that is where we have seen much of the activity around the movement happen, especially in American schools, often as a way of helping to keep school libraries relevant and vibrant in these changing times. You will also learn how to make the most of your makerspace by leveraging the resources you have available to you to create your own robust and unique learning environment within your library, classroom, or school.

We know well that the 21st-century global knowledge economy demands attributes of our workforce that are very different from earlier times. To thrive and succeed in today's turbulent times, people are required to be able to demonstrate high levels of imagination, of creativity, and of innovative thinking if they are continually to invent and manage new and better services and products for the global marketplace (Trilling & Fadel, 2009). Arising directly out of this worldwide ferment, we can see the invention and dissemination of makerspaces as one of the most exciting movements in education today. It is a movement that, at once, fuses two critical aspects of life today. On the one hand, it draws upon the innately human desire to make things using our hands and our brains, using tools, some of which we have used since the dawn of history, using materials provided by nature and by science, and using language too of course. And on the other hand, it draws inspiration from the broadest range of activities from across the digital sphere.

It was from the digital arena that the first digital makerspaces began to spread throughout Europe and North America in the early 2000s. Also referred to as FabLabs or Hackerspaces, they began in the mid-1990s in Germany as collectives of programmers and "hackers." Soon after that, makers began to extend the concept beyond the digital and into the fundamentals of making as an innately human capability. As a result, they then established the first fledgling spaces in New York, Washington D.C., and San Francisco (Matus, 2014). As a result, we now see a growing trend for schools to include a place where learners have the opportunity to explore their own interests, to tinker, create, invent, and build, using the widest variety of tools and materials. This Maker Movement is continually shaped and evolved by the variety of forces and influences playing on it: by its highly social and bottom-up history and heritage, by the multiplicity of educational purpose and rationales promoted by individual educators, and by the students' own creativity within the spaces themselves.

John Dewey, the father of American progressive education, once wrote, "Tools are the expression of the man/environment interaction; by their way, the means and the consequences of action are adapted to each other" (Hickman, 2009, p. 101).

Dewey believed that, through the use of tools, we humans have been able to enhance the world around us and to mitigate some of the constraints imposed on us by nature. Education, he concluded, had to allow children to flourish in an environment in which they could experience and interact with nature, with tools, with each other, and with the curriculum. Children had to participate actively in their own learning, with the teacher taking the role of a partner, a guiding influence, in that process.

But Dewey's understanding of "tools" went far beyond tangible objects, seeing personal attributes, shared ideas, organizations, and social institutions as part of the "technologies" we deploy in our interactions with each other. And the most important of them all, for Dewey, was language—he called it "the tool of tools" (Hickman, 2009). Our means of communication, going beyond merely the spoken and written word, are critical to our capacity as human beings to cooperate with each other, learn from each other, work with each other, and live effectively with each other.

Today, I feel that John Dewey would look kindly on the Maker Movement as a determined attempt to promote learning-through-doing in an open, social, and peer-led environment. Bringing the Maker Movement into schools and deploying the culture of fun, self-fulfillment, and a sharing of ideas and activities immediately allows children and young people to come together in a space that eschews the traditionally siloed curricular domains; that puts the learner firmly at the center of the learning; that enables teachers to encourage a much more participatory approach for students; and that often, it has to be said, encourages teachers out of their teacher-directed shells to experiment with the kinds of learner-focused activities that the makerspace fosters.

With Dewey's broad definition of tools in mind, I know that I came to the Maker Movement, not from a STEM orientation, but from a starting point in literacy. For years in my library, I had often created opportunities for my students to play and tinker with their reading and writing, with their efforts to communicate their ideas, to tell stories and to create narratives that were meaningful and significant to them. As a library media specialist, I felt I had the scope and the affordances to make that possible, to enable activities that often fell somewhere outside of or somewhere between the standard set of subject disciplines in the school curriculum. I realized in time that those early experiences were my first attempts to create a maker culture in my library; they were the start of a process that led me eventually to set up the makerspace in New Milford High School, New Milford, New Jersey.

All good teachers today have to acknowledge that they are also learners, and setting up a makerspace in your library is a great way to ensure that you, the teacher, not only can learn new things from the space but can do so openly with your students, to let them see you and respect you as a learner just like them! The makerspace encourages teachers to say to their students, we are all learners now, let's learn together!

CHAPTER

1

The Maker Movement

"Knowledge emerges only through invention and re-invention, through the restless, impatient, continuing, hopeful inquiry human beings pursue in the world, with the world, and with each other."

—Paulo Freire

To define a school makerspace by its purpose in the simplest of terms, it is a place where young people have an opportunity to explore their own interests; learn to use tools and materials, both physical and virtual; and develop creative projects. It should be envisaged and implemented as a concept that can adapt to a wide variety of uses, shaped not only by educational purposes defined by teachers or the school or the wider curriculum but also by students' own creative goals and interests. With a real potential to revolutionize education, we have begun to see makerspaces popping up all across the country.

The Chattanooga Public Library in Tennessee created a 14,000 sq. ft. space covering the whole of their 4th floor that is part-public-laboratory-part-edu-space. The Westport Library, in Westport, Connecticut, has a makerspace which serves very well as a model to be emulated and learned from in this new wave of library services. The space includes a 3-D printer and hosts presentations and participatory workshops on topics ranging from robotics to arts and crafts. At the Fayetteville Free Library in New York, they have not one but three makerspaces:

- Creation lab—focusing on digital creation
- Fab lab—focusing on the fabrication of tangible objects
- Little makers—offering a free play area that encourages children to create, imagine, and build.

At the Allen County Public Library in Fort Wayne, Indiana, they set up a makerspace that they call a Tekventure Maker Station, which is actually in a trailer outside the library. It houses a number of hand, power, and electronic tools for school use but also for the use of the community beyond the school.

All of these fine examples of the Maker Movement, and there are countless others across the country that deserve a mention too, are rooted in the idea of a "Participatory Culture," a term coined by American media scholar Henry Jenkins (Jenkins, Clinton, Purushotma, Robison, & Weigel, 2006). Jenkins recognizes the key elements of a participatory culture to include low barriers to expression and engagement, strong support for creating and sharing one's creations with others, and some type of informal mentorship whereby what is known by the most experienced is passed along to novices. That core idea of sharing one's creations is also reminiscent of something that Ivan Illich (1973) wrote in *Tools for Conviviality*:

> Tools are intrinsic to social relationships. An individual relates himself in action to his society through the use of tools that he actively masters or by which he is passively acted on. To the degree that he masters his tools, he can invest the world with his meaning. (p. 34)

Illich encouraged the use of what he termed "convivial tools," namely those that offer each of us opportunities to enrich our environment with the fruits of our own vision. Such tools are quite different from the passive tools that render us as "consumers" of their output, as recipients of meaning determined by others, and that deny us the power to use our own creativity to construct our own meaning in life.

Fundamentally, therefore, the Maker Movement is about moving from consumption to creation and turning knowledge into action. In pedagogical terms, it is firmly located within the broadly constructivist philosophies of education.

consumption ⟹ creation

While the idea of making is certainly not new, today's makerspaces are rooted firmly in the 21st century, in the here and now. They are of their time! They are a mash-up of differentiated learning experiences combining traditional elements supported by new technologies. The maker approach to learning is highly learner-driven and recognizes that while immediate and teacher-defined learning certainly does occur most of the time, it should not be the primary objective. One of the overriding themes in maker education is individuality. For the student to be given productive opportunities to shape his or her environment through making is a critical element in helping each of them to define his or her individuality within a social and sharing context. Their individuality within such an environment comes out of the solutions that students create and from the self-confidence and self-awareness that come from the process of designing, making, and sharing.

> The Maker Movement is about moving from consumption to creation and turning knowledge into action.

In my opinion, maker education is an organic movement that has gained particular traction in the United States since the adoption and implementation of the Common Core State Standards. It has been the great equalizer within, and in some ways against, our modern education system by allowing opportunities for informal learning to take place. Most learning in the makerspace happens casually, and even most intentional learning that happens there is not the result of programmed instruction (Illich, 1973). The effective use of educational makerspaces forms the basis for a paradigm shift in education that in many ways is a throwback to earlier educational systems that included programs like industrial arts and craftsmanship, but with a very modern twist, namely a renewed emphasis on informal learning. Our education system, I feel, has to recognize that informal learning should by no means be perceived any longer as irrelevant or in any way secondary to formal learning. As Frank Coffield (2000), professor of education at the Institute of Education in London, has written:

> Informal learning is not an inferior form of learning whose main purpose is to act as the precursor of the main business of formal learning. It is fundamental, necessary and valuable in its own right.

Quite elusive by nature and difficult to pin down, we should be nonetheless clear that informal learning opportunities for our students can inspire innovation and increase student performance in formal educational settings. As Eric Schmidt, the ex-CEO of Google, says, virtually everything new seems to come from the 20 percent of their time they give to their engineers to spend on side projects (The 70 Percent Solution, 2005).

In most people's minds, the Maker Movement in education is associated most often with STEM-related concepts and technology-based activities. There is good reason for that. However, my entry point into the makerspace movement came from a different route altogether, and it is important to recognize that there are many equally valid routes into the movement. I came to it primarily through the unusual route of literacy.

For years, in my library, I had often allowed opportunities for my students to play and tinker with their reading and writing.

A favorite of mine that I have used in this way is the digital story *Inanimate Alice*, written by Kate Pullinger and produced by Ian Harper (2005). This "born-digital" story has an "open text" construction and deliberately allows opportunities for student co-creation. My students enjoyed creating their own next episodes in the series by crafting their own narratives, using various tools and resources, both print and digital, or even remixing the *Inanimate Alice* assets to tell an original story. Another story I used to move my students through the continuum of creating, but with literacy as the inspiration, was *Skeleton Creek*, written by Patrick Carman (2009). This hybrid text is told half in print and half in video. Similar to *Inanimate Alice*, at the heart it tells stories across multiple media platforms. This transmedia story helped to move my students from consumption to creation and sparked a mash-up of differentiated learning experiences. Students designed multimedia reading experiences that fused story with video, games, and puzzles. Those early experiences were my first attempts at "making" in my library even though they were seemingly far removed from the usual conception of making with tools in the physical realm.

After years of experiences in playing with story in informal ways, I decided to take all these concepts and formalize them into a makerspace learning experience at a Mozilla Maker Party—one of hundreds of events around the world where people become active makers of the world around them. At the event, kids had the opportunity to create online comics, design video games, make stop-motion animation, and many other activities designed to unlock their creative potential. It was after this event that I decided to designate an area in my library as my makerspace. A string of highly imaginative literary experiences had led up to this and had therefore set the stage for creativity and making.

The Maker Movement encourages a growth mindset, which tolerates risk and failure and maybe even encourages it. It is a truism that is nonetheless rarely acknowledged in formal education that failure is a necessary step on the road to success and innovation. In the words of developmental psychologist and philosopher Jean Piaget, "When you teach a child something you take away forever his chance of discovering it for himself." Learning through mistakes is very much encouraged. This seemingly novel but in fact long-cherished approach to solving problems encourages our learners to try things they are interested in or to develop unknown capabilities. Steve Jobs taught us all that making mistakes and even failing can sometimes end up being the best things that ever happen to you.

The Maker Movement embraces the power of collaboration. The collaborative environment of a makerspace allows an individual to embrace and even seek out challenges beyond his or her comfort zone. Together, students can collectively engage in shared learning experiences. Students today are already aware that learning extends beyond the four walls of a school and they are part of a global educational community. This knowledge feeds directly into the networked learning that the Maker Movement allows for. Proponents argue that the networked aspect is a key distinction between this and earlier construction-centered affinity groups, such as a local woodwork or sewing club. Today's equivalent, the makerspace, offers far wider spheres of communication and enables a critical mass of learning to be achieved globally rather than necessarily locally (Sharples et al., 2013). Again, this speaks to and in creating a participatory culture where members feel some degree of social connection with one another (Jenkins et al., 2006).

This new and exciting Maker Movement is one that all educators need to embrace. In a recent piece written by Sylvia Libow Martinez and Gary Stager (2013), they pointed out what lessons educators need to embrace in light of this movement. They include the following:

- "Doing" is what matters
- Openness
- Give it a go
- Iterative design
- Aesthetics matter
- Mentoring defies ageism

- Learning is intensely personal
- It IS about the technology
- Ownership

By nature, the idea of making is playful. Tinkering is a uniquely human activity, combining social and creative forces that encompass play and learning (Kolk, 2011). At the high school level in particular, we tend to lose that playful spirit that we all know so well gets kids so engaged in whatever they are doing. I have seen firsthand in my library how receptive students are to having time for play as a part of their school day. If play is what you do outside school, then that is where the real learning will take place and that's where innovation and creativity will be found (Hlubinka et al., 2013). Dr. Stuart Brown has called this "neoteny," defined as the retention of immature juvenile qualities into adulthood and most assuredly an orientation that is a critical component of innovative thinking and real creativity in young people and adults. We need to find ways to bring that same spirit into school and to keep it there. The makerspace can help in that objective.

Research shows that play builds social-emotional competence in many domains: language skills, social skills, empathy, imagination, self-control, persistence, and higher-order thinking. Many argue that our focus on academic achievement has been at the expense of valuable play-based programs. The Maker Movement may be a way of bringing play back into the picture (Jackson, 2014).

Planning Your Makerspace

"There are two ways of being creative. One can sing and dance. Or one can create an environment in which singers and dancers flourish."

—Warren Bennis

Schools are already filled with creativity. The challenge is effectively cultivating it and harnessing it to its fullest. Laying a foundation for innovation will allow everyone to take full advantage of what a well-planned makerspace can provide. A simple makerspace that sparks the hearts and minds of students will invariably succeed whereas a fully adorned makerspace that lacks that spirit is certain to fail. Thus when considering the installation of a makerspace in school, it is crucial to first consider creating the culture and environment necessary for success.

Evidence suggests we should challenge our beliefs about creative, innovative thinking and the environments in which that thinking is fostered (Root-Bernstein & Root-Bernstein, 1999). For innovation to flourish, a carefully crafted environment built on trust, empowerment, and risk taking must be established. For those looking to plan their own makerspace, don't underestimate how "personal" the space needs to be. Rather than buying prepackaged kits or a makerspace in a box, better favored is a custom approach in creating a dynamic makerspace. While the instinct of many is to order the technology and the materials first, it is the planning that takes the most time and focus.

No two makerspaces should be the same. Understanding the needs, wants, and interests of your students and wider school community is an integral part in planning your space and ensures it will be a unique learning environment that will best serve your learners. Guided by the interests already inherent to your school will guarantee that your makerspace will be relevant and meaningful. This approach should take top priority over the tech and the tools.

In designing a makerspace for my library, I spoke at length with the students of New Milford High School about their creative interests and spent time just observing them on the computers and their devices at school. Talk to your students. They are your stakeholders. Invite students to discuss their interests and share their opinions. This model of integrated decision making, focused on the goal of maximizing the impact of your makerspace, will help to ensure a student-centered learning environment.

Gaining a deeper understanding of your school community will deepen the impact of your makerspace. In planning the makerspace for my school, along with communicating with my students, I also looked closely at the existing curricula, programs, and offerings. Based on all my findings, I then moved on to developing a number of themes that filled in gaps in the school's offerings and that extended STEM/STEAM-related concepts beyond the classroom wall, making them accessible for all.

Collaboration and networking are key principles related to contemporary makerspaces. When planning your makerspace, it is important to reach out to members of the greater maker community. Look closely at best practices from one makerspace to another. In planning my makerspace, I also examined the ever-changing landscape of global technology trends to find some that would be new and cutting edge to the entire school community.

After the planning process is complete, overarching themes for your makerspace are ready to be developed. The themes for my makerspace included the following:

- Robotics
- 3-D Printing/Design
- Hacking/Remixing the Web/Coding/Computer Programming
- Molecular Gastronomy
- Wearable Tech
- Electricity/Papertronics
- Polymers
- Engineering Inventions

The tools you select for your makerspace should inspire and allow for an environment rich with possibilities. After developing themes for your makerspace, it is finally time to order equipment and materials to support your themes. The items I ordered for my makerspace included the following:

- Legos—Architectural, Simple Machines
- Raspberry Pi
- 3-d Makerbot Printing Station
- Makey Makey Kits
- littleBits
- Arduino Boards
- Molecular Gastronomy Kits

- Robot Kits

- Papertronics

- Wearable Technology Items

In planning a makerspace, the technologies, resources, and materials around us and how they can be leveraged to engage and reach our learners need to be considered. These critical factors will ensure that your makerspace will be successful in encouraging meaningful student learning. Crucial to this is the deliberate creation and cultivation of a culture of innovation for all students. While this planning phase is incredibly important, driving real change means spending less time planning and more time doing.

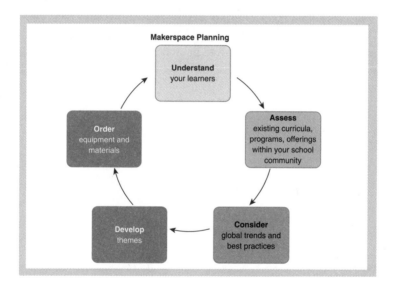

I have seen an adoption curve with establishing makerspaces. Many librarians are either not sure if they have the right resources, schedule, and budget or are reluctant to manage a space that includes activities that they might feel they are not experts in. One thing I cannot emphasize enough is to not be afraid of including things in your space that are new to you. Prior to establishing my makerspace, I had never used a 3-D printer nor did I feel I was proficient in electronics or robotics. The beauty of a space like ours is that it really has been a collective effort. I have learned as much from the students as they have learned from me and they have learned from each other. Use the resources that are within your means and what you have access to and put them into your space.

It is not necessary to be a technical expert to start a makerspace in your school or library. Many makerspaces are stocked with technologies such as 3-D printers. Many hesitate on bringing such technologies to their school because there is a feeling experts are required in order to teach such things. This is not strictly true. Some expertise may be needed to use certain tools common in makerspaces, but in general, educational makerspaces do not need to be overly complicated or formidable.

> If you build it, they will come and if you let them build it, they will learn.

CHAPTER
3

Setting Up Your Makerspace

After deciding upon the themes you want to advance in your makerspace and procuring the necessary equipment to support each theme, attention can be given to designing the physical aspects of the makerspace. A good place to start this process is to think about your institution's vision and strategy for learning (Higher Education Funding Council for England, 2006) and then to think through how your learning spaces can be seen as a physical representation of that strategy. It is also important, however, given the origins and motivations behind the makerspace movement, to seek to take that vision and strategy to a new level where you can. In the words of elementary principal and digital leader Brad Gustafson (2014), in setting up your makerspace, it is your task to set up the conditions for a new learning paradigm built upon innovation, creation, and design-iterations/failure to facilitate authentic learning. As the architect of your makerspace, the space you design should be open and welcoming, and invite exploration. You can't be sure of exactly how your makerspace will be used or what will take place in it, but that is just fine because you are creating the environment that will allow for creativity to flourish.

Practical considerations for setting up your makerspace include the following:

- Finding or creating a space with all the right utilities
- Making sure that the space has plenty of electrical outlets conveniently placed to reduce or eliminate extension cords
- Ensuring good network accessibility with plenty of network nodes and/or an effective Wi-Fi network
- If the choice of tools involves messy pursuits, then including sinks along with easily cleaned work surfaces and hard floors is optimal, but not necessary

No matter the source, fundamentally, the space should feel inspiring.

Perhaps the most important guiding principle in designing your space is to invite and make use of input from your students. The learner-focus of a makerspace must be more than mere rhetoric or sloganizing; it is absolutely critical to take into account the interests of those for whom the makerspace is primarily created. Allowing your students to become agents of change helps to create and ensure a dynamic, student-centered space. If you let them see that you are taking their views seriously and that they are making a difference, they will become your best marketers and advertising agents, all of which helps to ensure the vibrancy of your space.

The makerspace at my school has very much a DIY feel. It isn't slick or fancy looking in any way, but that unadorned feel has somehow fostered real creativity and innovative activity on the part of the students. To set up our physical space, I used my school's existing resources, including some library tables and bookshelves. Architecting the space was very much a collective effort and, having shared my plans with the school community,

I received great input from the school's tech team, I had access to the skills of the custodians, and I had an enthusiastic group of students who were interested in "making" experiences, and who were eager to see a place like this in their school and, therefore, wanted to contribute. By the end of this initial process, the physical makerspace ended up being a simple but effective learning environment that encouraged creativity and ideas by the design and construction of a wide variety of 3-D artifacts.

The layout of our makerspace consists of "fixed" stations and "flexible" stations. The fixed stations are areas that are out in the makerspace all the time for students to just walk in, sit down at, and engage with. These include the following:

- A littleBits Bar where students have the opportunity to participate in using modular electronics to invent their own creations
- A Take-Apart Tech Station, or "breaker space," where computers are provided and designated for students specifically to disassemble and investigate and to build
- A Lego table in which students can bring STEM concepts to life
- A Makey-Makey station, which allows students to turn any object into a game controller
- A 3-D Design and Printing station to make their designs and ideas a reality

In choosing these to be our fixed stations, I aimed to include activities that students would be able to start and complete during their time-limited visits to the space as well as to enable them to do so independently with little or no instruction needed.

Also included in the design of my makerspace are some "flexible" stations. These include activities that rotate in and out of the space or are things that can be uplifted and taken to classrooms for collaboration with classroom teachers during more formalized instruction sessions. Some examples of this from my makerspace include molecular gastronomy, robotics, and electric circuitry.

FIGURE 3.1 Take-Apart Tech Station

FIGURE 3.2 littleBits Bar

FIGURE 3.3 3-D Printing and Design

FIGURE 3.4 Makey-Makey Station

FIGURE 3.5 Lego Table

One of the highlights of the makerspace at New Milford High School is our Smart TV. Each day, I display on the Smart TV something I call a "Digital Breadcrumb," a puzzle or a task or an activity designed to challenge and provoke. I use these eye-catching displays and high-interest activities to draw students into the makerspace. Sometimes this might include playing a virtual musical instrument or playing a game of some kind. More often than not, students who have never visited the makerspace before are drawn in by this and, after engaging with our Smart TV, find themselves in the middle of the makerspace exploring some of the other activities in the space.

Space limitations, budgets, and policies often set hard limits to the design of a makerspace but do not need to limit what can be done. Inspiration need not be expensive. Overcoming such challenges offers opportunities to be creative. I firmly believe that anybody can create a makerspace on any budget and in any environment. Makerspaces can be low tech or high tech and can even be stocked entirely with secondhand materials and supplies. Look around you

FIGURE 3.6 Smart TV

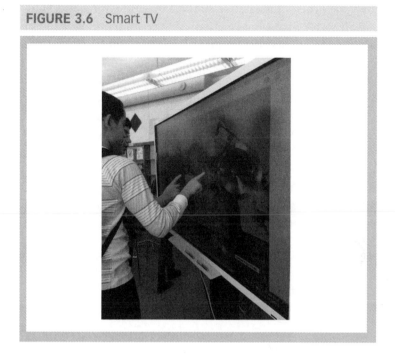

and use as many of the resources that you might already have available to you in your library, or ask for donations and look for grants. For those in spaces that are not able to be altered to accommodate a makerspace, consider the idea of a pop-up makerspace where, even on a movable cart, you can provide opportunities for students to create.

This is what Diana Rendina did for her makerspace at the Steward Middle Magnet School in Hillsborough County, Florida. She didn't have a lot of physical space to commit to one, so she knew that she'd have to start small. When she shared her vision with the other teachers in her school, she learned from the lead science teacher that the science department had several bins of K'nex and Legos gathering dust in a storage room. Diana cleaned them off, and with the coaxing of the Twitter community she created a pop-up makerspace. She put a couple of tables together in the library and left the bins out for the students to tinker with. The reaction from her students was amazing! They immediately starting experimenting and building all sorts of amazing creations. As the students gained interest, the pop-up makerspace grew. It began to spill out into other parts of the library. One table in a corner had a Snap Circuits set purchased through DonorsChoose, where students could experiment with electrical circuits. An art cart was rolled out during lunch breaks for students to decorate bookmarks, create designs with Perler beads, and make rainbow loom bracelets. Since all these activities were in bins or on carts, they could be moved out of the way whenever there were classes or events in the media center. The portability of their makerspace made it possible for making to happen in the library even though constrained by lack of space.

In many schools, makerspaces have popped up in places that were once used for something else. This is the case in the Van Meter Community School Library.

FIGURE 3.7

Photograph by Shannon McClintock Miller

Shannon McClintock Miller, district teacher librarian, decided to repurpose the library office that sat between the elementary and secondary libraries within her school. Once used for processing books, storing library materials, and typing up catalog cards, it was now needed by the school community for different reasons. With a Makerbot 3-D printer, Sphero's, and other maker materials taking over the office, Shannon, along with the students at Van Meter, decided to let it happen and just change the office to the maker-space they definitely needed within their library.

After the library associate Diana Hockenberry cleared out all the things that had been there for the last 20 years, Shannon empowered the young people to create their own makerspace. They drew up plans, made wish lists of materials that would fill the space, and gathered input from students and teachers alike. A group of seventh graders worked with Chriss Barr, the industrial technology teacher, to create a unique piece of furniture to fill the space in front of the windows across one wall of the room. The best part of this process was when the kids went around Van Meter measuring the shortest and tallest students in order to make sure the counter tops fitted the needs of everyone. Two seniors installed the counters and shelves, truly turning the office into a place where everyone could create, make, play, and have fun.

To walk into the library and see that small room busy with so much activity and happiness brought a lot more to the Van Meter School than a library office ever could. It fit the needs and voice of the young people. It not only gave them a voice and a chance to influence their own school's direction, but also showed that their learning and creativity could create real change within the library, across the whole school, and beyond the walls of the school as well.

Creating a Maker Culture in Your School

"I believe this passionately: that we don't grow into creativity, we grow out of it. Or rather, we get educated out of it."

—Sir Ken Robinson

A makerspace is, at one level, a relatively formalized workshop-like space but we can also view the concept of a makerspace as a metaphor for a place that encourages tinkering, play, and open-ended exploration for all students. It is an environment that emphasizes the importance of openness and sharing within and beyond the school and, in many ways, a place that encourages us to move beyond formal learning and curricular structures. Amongst the many innovations listed in the Open University's *Innovating Pedagogy Report* from 2013 is the notion of creating and nurturing a "maker culture" and it is this idea that is critical to our understanding of the effectiveness of our maker-spaces. The affordances offered by the digital technologies and by social media allow for enhanced opportunities to create a "maker culture" in schools like never before: It is a culture that emphasizes informal, networked, peer-led, and shared learning motivated by fun and self-fulfillment (Sharples et al., 2013).

It is my belief that every child has the right to invent, tinker, create, innovate, make, and do. This belief is what drove my mission to establish a makerspace at New Milford High School. The makerspace should be indifferent to distinctions such as academic potential, social barriers, and even levels of language development, and I have seen our makerspace successfully transcend all those standard differentiators of learners in our schools. Students of all levels can take full advantage of the resources and activities in this space. I often see students taking it upon themselves to help their peers and to inspire their peers to experiment, make, and do. Our space can be filled with our engineering and conceptual physics students at one moment, and then our English language learners and special-needs students at another, and often all at the same time. We truly have, I believe, democratized the tools and skills necessary to design and make things that are of interest to our students while, at the same time, we have exposed them all to a whole new world of possibilities. Our makerspace is about creating a genuine and committed culture of innovation, as well as about providing the foundation that the students need to be able to thrive and flourish in that kind of culture, one that is increasingly important in the economic life of our country.

Traditional education's focus on facts, memorization, basic skills, and test taking has been damaging to the development of creativity and innovation (Robinson & Aronica, 2009). In contrast, the maker culture embodies opportunities for experimentation and innovation, and as this DIY ethos has spilled into schools, it has reminded educators how much students can learn when they use their hands (Rix, 2014). The maker culture has attracted the interest of educators concerned about students' disengagement from STEM subjects in formal education settings (Sharples et al., 2013).

Not only is my makerspace overrun with students during their lunch periods, but teachers have come to realize how much the idea of making can enhance the wider learning experiences for the students in their classes. The concepts and principles of "making" have begun to spill into classrooms giving students authentic learning opportunities that go beyond their typical classroom experiences.

The Partnership for 21st Century Skills (n.d.) has pointed out that a focus on creativity, critical thinking, communication, and collaboration is essential to prepare students for the future. They say that students should be able to do the following:

- Think Creatively
  - ○ Use a wide range of idea creation techniques—such as brainstorming
  - ○ Create new and worthwhile ideas—both incremental and radical concepts
  - ○ Elaborate, refine, analyze, and evaluate their own ideas in order to improve and maximize creative efforts

- Work Creatively With Others
  - ○ Develop, implement, and communicate new ideas to others effectively
  - ○ Be open and responsive to new and diverse perspectives; incorporate group input and feedback into the work
  - ○ Demonstrate originality and inventiveness in work and understand the real-world limits to adopting new ideas
  - ○ View failure as an opportunity to learn; understand that creativity and innovation are a long-term, cyclical process of small successes and frequent mistakes
  - ○ Implement innovations
  - ○ Act on creative ideas to make a tangible and useful contribution to the field in which the innovation will occur

Establishing a culture of creation within a school goes far beyond just creating a makerspace, as demonstrated masterfully by Andy

Plemmons in the Barrow Media Center in Athens, Georgia. His work has shown that a physical room stocked with tools is an important part of the process, but even more significant is the objective of allowing creating to make its way into the mindset of students, educators, and families within the school. The best and most effective makerspaces will be found in schools in which goals, school improvement plans, and professional learning are developed in such a way as to foster a genuine culture of risk taking. This is a culture in which failure is welcome because that very failure is where the richest learning experiences take place. When students and teachers fail, they become more comfortable with the feeling of pausing, stepping back, re-evaluating the situation, and trying again. Students develop a mantra of never giving up and begin to support one another in trying new endeavors and figuring dilemmas out. Educators must give themselves and their students permission to slow down the fast-paced world of education and spend time dreaming, tinkering, creating, and sharing those creations with the world. Andy has learned that when educators step back and allow students to tinker, miraculous things happen. Students who have been disconnected from school suddenly find their niche. Not only that, students become problem solvers and inventors. They naturally exhibit the higher-order thinking skills that educators spend many fruitless hours trying to teach through traditional instruction.

Setting up a makerspace, or even just having maker tools within a school, offers teachers, students, and families an opportunity to experience tinkering and creating, and it is precisely these kinds of tools that are new and unfamiliar to most learners. When all learners, no matter their previous achievements, jump into something new, it has the effect of levelling the playing field. It is that levelling process that allows expertise to grow organically within the group and then to spread naturally across the group through excitement, conversation, and the showcasing of creations. Educators and students can work together to brainstorm how these tools and possibilities flow within the constraints of standards and mandates in education. When a culture of creation begins to be established, the energy of all learners drives the desire to dream, tinker, create, and share every day in multiple content areas. The culture then flows out from the makerspace and into regular classrooms, libraries, and classes such as art and music. A culture of creation encourages learners to identify the challenges of the world and to seek and create solutions. Our students hold a wealth of knowledge and ideas. Educators just need to open the landscape of learning to all so that their knowledge is able to come forth.

Indeed teachers can themselves find new challenges and learning opportunities with maker technology and they can begin to embrace a new pedagogy that embraces the enthusiasm and attitude of the Maker Movement (Martinez & Stager, 2014). The focus becomes less on the construction of objects and more on the social, shared learning experiences created by the learners themselves. Risk taking is encouraged in the form of allowing learners to push their skills outside of their comfort zone, allowing for real skill progression. Creativity and innovation can be nurtured by learning environments that foster questioning, patience, openness to fresh ideas, high levels of trust, and learning from mistakes and failures (Trilling & Fadel, 2009). Clear-thinking and confident educators can discover ways to blend maker skills into the core curriculum. This can be as easy as making use of a platform such as DIY.org for students to help them discover skills and share what they make and do with each other and across a global community. Through this platform, teachers can explore skill-based learning and introduce collaboration into their classrooms.

Makerspaces and the Standards

" . . . the [Common Core] standards are . . . open to allowing educators to keep what works and find new approaches to fix what doesn't. We need to make sure our classes are balanced between creativity, critical thinking, and career skills, for all of these things are vitally important for a life well lived."

—Ashley Lauren Samsa, guardian.com

Many teachers in America believe that we face a dilemma: teaching to the plethora of standards we are asked to adhere to, or pursuing worthy long-term intellectual goals (Wiggins & McTighe, 2007). I do not believe this dilemma is a real one, for the simple reason that the two are simply not mutually exclusive. It is more than possible to do both, to improve teaching and learning by aligning the practice and formative development of skills and ways of thinking to the standards, and by means of a wide variety of creative and innovative pathways to learning. With just a little imagination and some professional planning, makerspaces can fit in perfectly well with the philosophy and learning goals of not only the Common Core State Standards, but also the International Society for Technology in Education (ISTE) Standards, and the American Association of School Librarian (AASL) Standards for the 21st Century Learner.

Rather than embodying any one learning goal, makerspaces offer an environment that allows students to develop many of the skills outlined in the standards. So while the makerspace in and of itself does not align to the standards, it is more than possible to create activities that align with many of the objectives of the standards. Take, for example, Lakewood City Schools in Lakewood, Ohio, who are really taking the makerspace very seriously indeed by designing, at the time of writing, a makerspace that will offer a full high school curriculum aligned with standards for their students. The curriculum, physical space, and community of learners will be centered on the concept of the makerspace, which will empower students to identify, articulate, and design solutions to real-world problems (Next Generation Learning Challenges Grant Recipients, 2014).

But such activities need not be teacher-led at all times—teachers should be encouraged to plan and work with their students to develop, jointly, activities that catch students' interests while, at the same time, enabling the teacher to use the activities to meet the required standards appropriate to age and subject. Tinkering and making are activities that can very effectively support a collaborative, iterative design methodology, where student-centered projects can be seen as a means of preparing students for real-world challenges in careers and college (Martinez & Stager, 2014). Through such activities we can nurture an improvement in higher-order thinking skills, such as problem solving, critical thinking, and creativity, all brought together in the kinds of interests and projects that can happen in a space where teachers and students are learning by making. For example, a carefully crafted unit on 3-D printing and design can have skills embedded in it that address several of the ISTE Standards for Students: Communication and Collaboration; Creativity and Innovation; Critical Thinking, Problem Solving and Decision Making; and Technology Operations and Concepts.

The work that takes place in makerspaces is as relevant to the AASL Standards for the 21st Century Learner as it is to the Common Core. Making is an inquiry-driven social activity that allows students to develop the very skills, dispositions, responsibilities, and strategies touted in the AASL's 21st Century Standards (Canino-Fluit, 2014). Both the AASL Standards and the Common Core emphasize the importance of independently reading informational texts in a variety of formats. To build a foundation for college and career readiness, students must read widely and deeply from among a broad range of high-quality, increasingly challenging literary and informational texts. By reading texts in history/social studies, science, and other disciplines, students build a foundation of knowledge in these fields that will also give them the background to be better readers in all content areas.

Students also acquire the habits of reading independently and closely, which are essential to their future success (Common Core State Standards Initiative, 2014). The texts students need to read in order to gain knowledge necessary to complete their maker projects present an excellent opportunity for students to meet these goals. Students are motivated as they push ahead with challenges in the makerspace, to do whatever research is needed, either from books or online, to help them complete their tasks successfully. In addition, important elements of the Maker Movement involve students collaborating on projects, seeking assistance, presenting, and explaining their projects and their processes of making at Maker Faires and showcases as well as during class time. This type of thinking blends very well indeed with many of the objectives of Common Core, especially when expanding into new iterations and new ideas.

I can offer an example of using the makerspace to promote standards. One of my favorite makerspace-related lessons involved collaboration with our Physics class. The class was aware of our littleBits bar and their teacher asked if he could bring his students into the makerspace for some hands-on experiences related to their electronics unit. Prior to their visit, students had worked with a pHET DC Circuit Simulator, which allowed them to explore current flows through light bulbs in circuits powered by batteries and controlled by switches. However, in the ideal scenarios presented by the simulator, the students missed out on practical issues such as low batteries, poor electrical connections, and other authentic experiences that impact circuits. This all changed dramatically when students were afforded a hands-on, real-world learning experience in the makerspace that allowed them to create real learning artifacts so that they could work toward conceptual mastery.

Once in the makerspace, students began to create, tinker, and invent to learn concepts related to circuitry. When they made circuits that rotated paper hands and another that created light-up shoes, they faced a number of challenges, but by working together, by sharing ideas, they were able to overcome all impediments and eventually experienced success. For example, they had to troubleshoot in order to find a broken lead on a connection to the battery or find an open circuit because a connection that appeared to be made was electrically disconnected. During this activity, as a formative assessment method, we had the students create an "exit slip" in which they had to diagram and explain the flow of electricity through their circuit.

This exit slip aligned to these standards:

- WORK.9–12.9.1.12.A.1, Apply critical thinking and problem-solving strategies during structured learning experiences.
- SCI.9–12.5.1.12.B.2, Build, refine, and represent evidence-based models using mathematical, physical, and computational tools.

Through our littleBits activity, students were able to extend their invaluable hands-on experiences to simulated circuits which presented the conditions for deriving Kirchoff's Laws for Series and Parallel circuits. Without this experience with power sources, current flow, and activation of elements—buzzers, lights, motors, etc.—they would have struggled with the more abstract simulated circuits. The makerspace is an ideal environment for bringing theory and practice together across a wide range of disciplines.

CHAPTER
6

The "Expert" Maker

"Authenticity—we know it works!"

—James Miller, Edutopia,
Bringing Authenticity to the Classroom

Maker culture resonates with the current interest in lifelong learning and in cross-generational learning, with skills transmitted not only from old to young but also from young to old (Sharples et al., 2013). One of the most significant events in my makerspace was a visit from Ron Grosinger, an expert maker who came into school to run a bicycle repair workshop for our students. The day he visited, our library was filled with eager students, along with their bikes, for the event. Participants were engaged and inspired, and on a different level than I had ever seen before in the space. Every single young person in the room that day participated actively and eagerly in the event. What I realized from this initiative was that, in addition to providing the physical spaces, we need to develop communities of interest that connect learners with mentors for the purpose of sharing knowledge about the tools and tinkering techniques (Balsamo, 2011). It emphasized for me the importance of having recognized experts visit maker-spaces to inspire innovation, passion, and personal motivation.

A hallmark of the Maker Movement is the inclusion of real experts who are able to demonstrate their skills for students and show those students first-hand that the skills they gain in the space have real-world applications. Ron's visit showed our students that makers can earn a living from their making, that real people can develop their making skills to the point where they can form the basis of a trade or a career, or even simply a pleasurable lifelong hobby. Seeing expertise transformed into a sellable skill, or a powerful life skill, is a critical lesson for our students to take away from a makerspace. Receiving a critical response to their own making attempts from a seasoned expert can be hugely valuable to the learner. Ron's visit spurred a new initiative for me that I call "Hangout With a Maker."

As a part of my initiative, I regularly call upon community members to visit our makerspace to demonstrate their skills and expertise. This includes individuals who have skills in a range of activities including robotics, cooking, textiles, engineering, electronics, 3-D design, mechanical repair, and much more—in short, making nearly anything! A wonderful resource for bringing experts into your makerspace is the Exploratorium Tinkering Studio (The Tinkering Studio, n.d.), which invites artists, scientists, educators, and jacks-of-all-trades to codevelop ideas and activities, and learn about new technologies. In the Tinkering Studio, your students can learn more about these tinkerers, their work, and their involvement.

Experts can also be peers who rise to the occasion and are eager to share their knowledge and newfound skills. Peer learning is extremely valuable, and must not be underestimated in providing support and encouragement to learning in the makerspace, but there is something special—some secret sauce—about experiencing the honed skills of the expert. As Ivan Illich wrote, "Someone who wants to learn knows that he needs both information and critical response to its use from somebody else" (Illich, 1971, p. 77).

My hope in introducing the expert makers into the makerspace is that such visits will empower our students not just to seek out jobs or develop lifelong interests in STEM or in other creative fields, but to think entrepreneurially and seek to make their own jobs and industries, depending on their interests. We have already begun to see the impact of this movement in our school since our makerspace has already begun to influence the college major choices of our seniors with real consequences for their future career paths.

Take, for example, Paige, a frequent visitor to our makerspace. As a senior, she often visited during her independent study periods or her lunch. Paige always had an interest in computer science, but says her time in our makerspace this year has helped her determine her college major and what she wants to do with her career. She said the makerspace played a big part in realizing how much she loves computers and technology and coming to an appreciation that her interest could turn into her career. Paige's favorite station in our space was our Take-Apart Tech Station where she had both taken apart computers and built them. As a result of the successful work she did at that station, and her passion for doing so, I arranged for Paige to work an internship with our technology department during the summer months. As a result of their mentorship, Paige decided to go to school for IT.

Paige's story is a real-world example of how the maker movement inspires innovation, passion, and personal motivation and interests. Students should be made aware of traditional science career options related to STEM disciplines, including chemistry, computer science, engineering, environmental science, geosciences, life sciences, mathematics, and physics/astronomy. They should also learn about more creative fields inspired by makerspaces such as film production, Legoland designer, professional hackers, 3-D fashion design, and molecular gastronomy.

It is wonderful to see students becoming empowered to seek out jobs, courses, and careers in makerspace-related fields. However, we also need to teach them that they can exercise initiative by organizing their own professional ventures. There is a powerful connection between making and career and technical education in terms of applied learning and entrepreneurship (Rix, 2014).

MAKERSPACE-INSPIRED CAREERS = SCIENCE + CREATIVITY + ENTREPRENEURSHIP

By nurturing the entrepreneurial spirit, students will see that they can create their own jobs and industries depending on their interests. For example, a group of our students spent a school year designing and creating 3-D printed items not only for themselves,

FIGURE 6.1 The makerspace forms a bridge between the community and the schools.

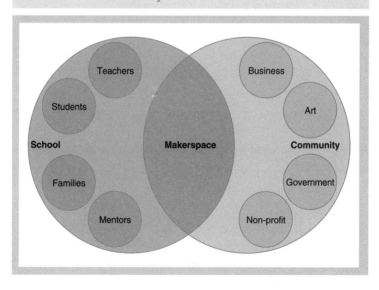

SOURCE: Makerspace @ Lakewood City Schools, 2014.

but also had lots of interest from their friends and family. Inspired by Amazon's 3-D printed items store, the students developed a plan for their own online store that will allow them to design, create, print, customize, and sell their own 3-D printed items.

A powerful component of the Maker Movement is initiating and supporting the formation of social relationships between mentors and learners. Our current education system struggles to tap the resources available in the community, yet our culture is richer with information and opportunities than ever before (Hlubinka, DeRose, Dougherty, Wilkenson, & Petrich, 2012). It is important, in this regard, to recognize that such mentors need not always be credentialed or certificated "experts"—an appreciation of the making skills of the self-taught and the gifted amateur can provide another important lesson in life for our students.

Fundamentally, we need to work with community members as true partners in maker-related learning initiatives. This shared commitment to open exploration, fostering creativity and making, significantly helps to push the Maker Movement forward and enriches the learning in school immeasurably.

CHAPTER

7

Makerspaces and the School Library

"Many libraries have found that maker culture and makerspaces fit naturally with their existing missions, and have begun to incorporate makerspaces into the services they offer their communities."

—Sharona Ginsberg, Instructional Technology Consultant, *Makerspaces: What Are They?*

The best school libraries are not just surviving; they are thriving in this new digital information environment, an environment that is typified, as Sharona Ginsberg notes above, not by the scarcity of knowledge resources that existed in the era in which public libraries were founded, but by a condition of knowledge abundance. The school libraries that are thriving recognize this profound shift and know they cannot continue to prosper without seriously repurposing their physical spaces to suit the changing times (Johnson, 2010). Creating makerspaces is undoubtedly one powerful way to ensure that school libraries remain relevant in the 21st century. Libraries are ideally situated to contribute to the development of the technological and creative imagination through the support of tinkering practices and the creation of mixed-reality make-spaces (Balsamo, 2011). The library has long been an engine for the democratization of knowledge and information, but we have to recognize today that a library's role is no longer simply about providing access to information. Libraries are open access by nature, and makerspaces can take advantage of such openness to create opportunities for partnership, collaboration, and creation for all. In a makerspace, as has always been the case in a library, curiosity and active community-based learning are front and center (Schwelm, 2014).

There are those who feel that the noise or mess produced by the activities and equipment that often accompany makerspaces can create challenges for libraries. It would be a shame if a school were to miss out on the amazing learning opportunities proffered by a makerspace simply because of a misguided wish to preserve the traditional concept of the quiet studious library from all change. It is our responsibility as school librarians to promote effective and purposeful learning in our libraries, not to preserve in aspic some golden-age notion of the library as a repository of books and little else. In any case, the idea of "making" in libraries has a long, rich history. As far back as 1873, in Gowanda, New York, the *Gowanda Ladies Social Society* came together to knit, sew, socialize, and talk about books. In 1905, Frances Jenkins Olcott, the children's department head at the Carnegie Library of Pittsburgh, helped to establish home libraries in working-class houses, where she organized crafts such as sewing or basketry for local kids. In 1933, the Manitoba (Canada) Crafts Museum and Library was created as a meeting place and resource to connect people to crafts while both preserving the province's cultural heritage and teaching students how to craft. In 1960, the Nebraska Public Library Commission hosted a variety of special activities, including creative arts that were organized by area groups. In 1976, we even saw in Columbus,

Ohio the first tool-lending library. From this idea of making, we have seen the birth of what is known as a "makerspace," which now seems to be the next step in library transformation in the 21st century (List of tool-lending libraries, n.d.).

And transformation it is! When I established the makerspace in New Milford High School, I started with the moderate hope that students, and perhaps even teachers, would see some value in the venture and would gradually make more and more use of it over time. How wrong I was! Almost from the day and hour we opened the makerspace, an incredible transformation took place in my high school. The library that I took guardianship of when I started in NMHS was, to put it mildly, a barren wasteland. It was, frankly, a dull, lifeless physical space with a sorry collection of outdated and barely opened books crowding the old shelves. Most critically of all, I took over a library that was bereft, most of the time, of the one thing that makes a school library what it is: learners! The library was largely empty for most of the school day.

That same library is now a thriving learning metropolis where students flock to tinker, invent, create, collaborate, work, and most importantly, learn. Modern-day libraries have to take a participatory approach to learning and creating, with the aim of making both the learning that goes in the library, and the school library itself, so much more relevant to learners. The library should always strive to be the beating heart of the school as a learning community. Making in the library is about offering students opportunities to move from simply being users and consumers to being creators, by providing them with the space, tools, and resources they need. Of course, the library is still a library—its role as a place to read, to research, and to access information has not been supplanted—not in the least! There is still a place for that traditional role, of course, but the library today is a place where knowledge is created and not merely consumed. So much of the learning that happens in the library today is not the result of instruction and not the result of students being led by the nose to read texts as directed by their teachers, but rather the result of unhampered participation in a meaningful setting, just as Ivan Illich (1971) suggested was a necessary condition for real learning nearly a half a century ago.

Examples of great library-based makerspaces abound. For example, Buncombe County Schools in Asheville, North Carolina transformed their school library media centers into flexible learning spaces earmarked by designs that encourage choice and voice for their students. At the core of their endeavor is a focus on access and the ability to create, make, and produce items that reflect students' interests (Parker, 2014).

Their goal is to create a "Four-C-Able" Space for the Foreseeable Future, based on the four Cs of 21st Century learning:

1. Creativity
2. Collaboration
3. Communication
4. Critical Thinking

The Buncombe County model is one that other libraries could, and should, emulate to great effect. Their approach shows us that, in addition to the Maker Movement being a revolution in learning, it allows us to further shape the role of a modern-day school library media specialist. Librarians who are willing to champion makerspaces—and more and more of my professional peers are doing just that—can serve as powerful agents of change in their school community by putting innovative practices in place, by experimenting to discover what works and what does not—and why—and by taking risks! Makerspaces in the school library can serve as the perfect starting point for reimagining the very important space we occupy in the school. The idea of making, while not new, has hit a real resurgence and is flourishing, and most especially in school libraries. Library Media Specialists have the scope and the affordances to enable activities that, in so many ways, step outside of the relative rigidity of the classroom canon; if my own makerspace is anything to go by, the rewards of doing so are simply spectacular.

CHAPTER
8

Makerspaces as a Unique Learning Environment

"We need pedagogy free from fear and focused on the magic of children's innate quest for information and understanding."

—Sugata Mitra

To support the unique learning needs of each child and to create the conditions in which 21st-century learning can best happen, we must be prepared to seek out and create new learning structures, tools, and relationships (Trilling & Fadel, 2009). I believe that makerspaces can help in this quest by giving us some much-needed scope to broaden the concept of traditional school-bound learning spaces to create unique, as well as uniquely adaptable, learning environments that our students need, want, and will flourish in. In New Milford High School, I found myself in a place of learning that was blessed with many highly professional, forward-thinking, and resourceful teachers pushing the boundaries of teaching practice, but even in such a rich environment, our makerspace was still able to give our students opportunities to explore altogether new ways of learning. It also offered my teaching colleagues many new opportunities to take their own teaching to new places and in new directions. The creation of our makerspace allowed us to transform our once largely irrelevant library into a vibrant media center that now serves as a wonderful learning hub, a unique, flexible, and highly configurable learning environment offering inspiration to our students within and beyond school.

As we have seen earlier in the book, the concept of the makerspace carries with it a culture that is teeming with the promise of a different kind of learning. The maker culture is undoubtedly flourishing and this presents us, as educators, with a great opportunity to distinguish the makerspace from other spaces in the school or larger community by making it different and inviting and compelling. By enabling a shift away from teacher-led, or even curriculum-led, instruction, maker education is able to inspire a deeper form of learning where self-organized, social, participative learning can be put into practice in both formal and informal contexts. At core the educational makerspace is based on student ownership of their learning. I have endeavored to ensure that my makerspace is very much learner driven, and capable of exploiting the idea of real, hands-on experiential learning. It is a veritable mash-up of differentiated learning experiences combining traditional elements, new technologies, a significant shift in the locus of control over learning, and a determined plunge into the turbulent but exciting waters of collaborative learning.

Aligned with a constructivist approach to learning, the line between teacher and learner in the makerspace becomes blurred. In this environment, the greatest respect the teacher can accord his or her students is to say, here we are all learners, let's learn together. For instance, I have had students with the confidence to take it upon themselves to unpack high-level tools and concepts related to 3-D printing and design, teach them to me, and teach them to their peers. In many other cases, I have watched as students collaborate to meet a wide variety of challenges for themselves while being actively engaged in learning and teaching new concepts to each other. It is a "teaching" process like no other, because the students naturally and automatically see themselves as both teachers and learners at once, often unconsciously, and they can slide from one to the other many times in a single session: at one moment they are all learning as a group, at another one member may take on a temporary teaching role when they feel confident they know something that their peers do not, and at others, there is a wonderful dialectic going on in which all are teaching and all are learning at the same time. On many such occasions I have been the facilitator for the students' learning, but on even more occasions I have simply been an observer, intervening only when further rigor or the need to pass on a gem of wisdom from experience became necessary.

The primary objective of a teacher in an ideal maker environment is to facilitate the acquisition of concepts—this requires the teacher to be prepared to take on a more complex and, it has to be said, more difficult role than would normally be the case in a normal classroom situation. With this pedagogical shift, meaningful student learning is encouraged through a combination of self-directed learning on the part of the student himself or herself, collaborative learning across the group where there is one, and the teachers deploying the full arsenal of methods and judgment at their professional disposal. A makerspace is a learning environment that encourages the instructional transformation of a learning space, and it is an environment that, in my experience, students and teachers want to be a part of. I have lost count of the number of times I have found myself waiting patiently, long after school officially finished for the day, as a handful or more of students try to get something completed that they started earlier in the day. Often they end up taking material and equipment home to finish their task, such is their enthusiasm and commitment to the learning they are involved in.

Sugata Mitra, Professor of Education at Newcastle University in England, has shown us through his work the power of curiosity to motivate independent learning. Inviting wonder and curiosity is an important consideration in the educational makerspace environment and just cannot be underestimated as a prime motivator of learning. Mitra's results over recent years have offered, for me, some of the most compelling evidence for the dynamic effects of curiosity on knowledge acquisition and on that fundamental individual and intrinsic motivation to learn (Hole-in-the-Wall, 2013). From such wonder and such curiosity comes a real desire to learn and to explore new knowledge, new concepts, and new territory of the mind. And indeed, encouraging playfulness can also help to ignite that curiosity. Effective educational makerspaces engage students through the medium of playfulness, something that can only be fully achieved in an environment without fear or undue compulsion. It is by no means only with the youngest learners that play lies at the core of innovation and creativity.

Maker education fosters curiosity, tinkering, and iterative learning, which in turn leads to better thinking through better questioning. I believe firmly that this learning environment fosters enthusiasm for learning, student confidence, and natural collaboration. Ultimately, the outcome of maker education and educational makerspaces leads to determination, independent and creative problem solving, and an authentic preparation for the real world by simulating real-world challenges. Makerspaces have helped us reenvision and redefine the concept and the processes of learning.

CHAPTER
9

Showcasing Student Creations

"Tell me and I forget, teach me and I may remember, involve me and I learn."

—Benjamin Franklin

A major component in the overall Maker Movement is the idea of a Maker Faire. A Maker Faire is an event originally created by Make magazine to "celebrate arts, crafts, engineering, science projects and the Do-It-Yourself (DIY) mindset" (Maker Faire, n.d.). These events are special because they are filled with interesting and diverse projects, and they bring hosts of smart, creative people together to share in the pleasure and passion of making. Maker Faires have become hugely popular and they are undoubtedly a critical player in creating a maker culture across the

United States and beyond (Hlubinka et al., 2013). I would encourage everyone who picks up this book to attend a Maker Faire, see for yourself what it's about, and experience the sheer exuberance of the occasion amidst the noise and bustle of making and showcasing. Even better, go that one big step further and really take the maker mindset on board by hosting one at your school.

We now see Maker Faires or Maker Parties popping up all over the country. But Maker Faires don't necessarily have to be physical events; they can also be held successfully online. Recently even the White House hosted its first Maker Faire online. Using the #NationofMakers hashtag, staff provided opportunities for celebrating involvement in the Maker Movement. Just drop the hashtag into Twitter's search box and you will instantly be immersed in a wonderful flurry of Fab Labs, enterprise links to making and building all kinds of physical and virtual artifacts, 3-D printing ideas, and a host of other exciting happenings in the world of making. Even NASA has gotten into the act (Lowery, 2014)! The White House was able to highlight and celebrate many remarkable stories of makers, and it was able to get many leading organizations involved to help more students and entrepreneurs get involved in making things.

My journey into this idea of making was at the Brooklyn Storymakers Maker Party organized by the Brooklyn Public Library and Hive NYC Learning Network. At the event, children had the opportunity to create online comics, design video games, make stop-motion animation, and engage in many other activities designed to unlock their creative potential. The event was part of a Mozilla Maker Party—one of hundreds of events around the world where people become makers. With the digital story *Inanimate Alice* (Pullinger & Harper, 2005) as our mentor text, I worked with students to create postcards that characters in the story might send to the main character Alice. Using the Mozilla Webmaker tool Thimble, kids remixed postcards using digital media and the Internet. The tool allowed the children to remix their favorite digital postcards by modifying HTML and cascading style sheets (CSS) right in their browser. Instantly, they were able to see the results of their work. Each postcard was written as a #25wordstory, a process of writing created by educator Kevin Hodgson (2010) that lent itself well to our activity. It was a wonderful introduction for me to the pleasures of the makerspace, and I was inspired by seeing so many children being not simply so creative but also willing and proud to share the results of their efforts through social media.

Even in the school makerspace, it is a great idea to draw from the principles of a Maker Faire by finding opportunities for your students to showcase, celebrate, and share their creations. This can all be enhanced and promoted through the creation of online spaces or by leveraging social media tools to give students a channel for displaying their work and telling others about what they have done. In today's world, of course, it is easy for such community interaction and knowledge sharing to be mediated through the social and networked technologies, with websites and social media tools forming the basis of knowledge repositories and a central channel for information sharing and exchange of ideas, enabling cooperative construction, peer feedback, and validation (Maker Culture, n.d.). By taking advantage of social media channels we can meet and showcase to people where they are.

Some examples might include the following:

- Tweet photos of student work. I tweet several times a day both to the #nmhs and #worldsofmaking hashtag on Twitter. Students know this and either I tweet about what they have done or they will even tweet about their creations themselves using the same hashtags. They are proud to know that they have a global audience and that their work is showcased on the Internet. Although the current generation of young people is already well aware of the power of the Internet, they still manage always to be amazed at how far their work travels.

- Take videos of your students in the space. I have a Vine Channel set up for our school's makerspace. Vine allows you to create short, high-quality, looping videos that can be shared through social media channels. These videos are a great way to tell your makerspace's story.

- Take photos of students in action as well as their creations. I post photos on our school library's Facebook page, I tweet them, post on Instagram, and share on Pinterest as well.

The key here is to take the twin-track approach of, on the one hand, enabling your students to showcase their work to each other and across the school community and, on the other hand, giving them online channels to let them put their creative efforts on display for an audience across the world. Proponents of the latter approach argue that the networked aspect is a key distinction between this and earlier construction-centered affinity groups, such as a local woodwork or sewing club. By extending the spheres of communication available to our students—and our teaching colleagues—we can begin to see the real and sustainable benefits they will garner from opening themselves up to that wider audience (Sharples et al., 2013).

A great place to start is at makerfaire.com, where they describe this global phenomenon of Maker Faires as "the greatest show and tell on Earth" (Maker Faire: A Bit of History, 2013)— a perfect description!

CHAPTER

10

Makerspaces as Catalysts for Future Change

"Be the change that you wish to see in the world."

—Mahatma Gandhi

According to the U.S. Department of Education, only 16 percent of American high school seniors are proficient in mathematics and interested in a STEM career. Furthermore, only half of those students who do actually pursue a college major in a STEM field then choose to work in a related career. As a nation, we are falling behind internationally, ranking 25th in math and 17th in science among industrialized nations (United States Department of Education, n.d.). This international slippage is happening at exactly the same time as we are watching an across-the-board explosion all over the country in the numbers of STEM-related jobs that our economy needs to fill. During this current decade between 2010 and 2020, while all other occupations taken together are projected to increase by around 14 percent, STEM-based jobs are increasing dramatically, from "just" a 16 percent rise in math-related careers to a huge 62 percent increase in biomedical engineering jobs.

The various STEM initiatives being championed by President Obama—the STEM Innovation Proposals, the STEM Innovation Network, the STEM Teacher Pathways, and the National STEM Master Teacher Corps—will surely begin to make a difference. But I believe that right here in our schools—today!—we can add to the effects of such top-down strategies by working from the bottom up, establishing makerspaces to encourage all our students, no matter what their interests or skill level might be, to begin to see links between the fun and enjoyment they experience while they

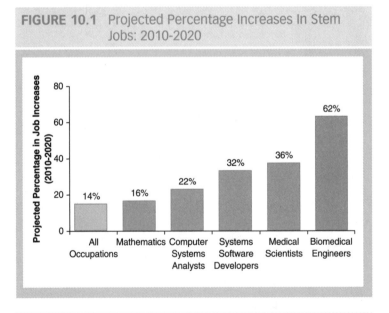

FIGURE 10.1 Projected Percentage Increases In Stem Jobs: 2010-2020

SOURCE: http://www.ed.gov/stem

are making and possible future careers in STEM. A makerspace will provide a powerful set of opportunities for students of any skill level to jump-start their STEM education, or even simply to discover if their interests lie in that direction.

It would be a mistake to dismiss the Maker Movement as just about 3-D printing and Legos; as I hope this book is showing, it should be clear by now that the makerspace is about much broader-based educational objectives and even reform. Over the past generation or so, we have seen how so many significant changes that have taken place within education have resulted from something that has disrupted the system from within. These have proven sometimes to have the biggest impact, often much bigger than external, top-down, policy-driven forces for change. Coming out of the grassroots, I firmly believe that makerspaces are more than capable of driving real and sustained systemic change from within the system. As Gary Stager, one of the world's leading experts and advocates for making in the classroom, says, making inspires education reform (Stager, 2014). That, in my opinion, has things exactly the right way around: real change has to come from within the system, from a growing recognition of the need for change in the schools and classrooms themselves.

Research has shown that students experience three gaps in their schooling: the expectations gap—where teachers have varying expectations of their students based sometimes on erroneous assumptions, as well as where students themselves have expectations of themselves that do not coincide with the expectations of their teachers; the relationships gap—where the quality of the relationship between teacher and student is not always as strong as it could or should be; and the participation gap—where there is a "gulf in opportunity and advantage between those few students who are actively engaged in their classes and the life of the school and the many others who are not." Every good teacher knows that student achievement and student opportunity are connected to the kinds of expectations, relationships, and chances for participation that students perceive they have in school (Quaglia, Fox, & Corso, 2010). Closing the education gap and raising achievement means having to find ways to close the participation gap by amplifying learning through innovative strategies. The Maker Movement is one powerful strand that offers such possibilities. The transformative potential of scaling up innovation and empowering our learners will position our students to be the central driving force of change in our schools. This can be done by the following:

- Involving students directly and as equal partners in developing your makerspace initiatives
- Creating a makerspace that has an atmosphere conducive to innovation and one that welcomes participation by making it okay to take risks
- Developing maker activities that target the interests of all students and particularly those that may thrive in more nontraditional learning environments
- Removing barriers by creating accessible opportunities where all students can learn new skills
- Embracing an open-source ideology, which will democratize access to tools and resources in your entire school community. Free web tools have made a wide variety of making experiences accessible to all.

The real work of a 21st-century education is to spark the passion for lifelong learning that our kids will need to navigate their way to a promising tomorrow (Institute of Play, 2014). Connecting students to the future requires changing the education system (Jenlink, 1995). The Maker Movement is tackling these issues head on and has already begun to transform learning in those schools that have established makerspaces that are sympathetic to all of the factors I hope are being brought out by this book. One of my hopes in developing my makerspace was that it would serve as a catalyst for future changes in the curriculum and in my school community, some of which, gratifyingly, I have already seen happen. I have seen classroom teachers begin to adjust their curricula and their teaching practice in order to reflect many of the principles related to making. I have seen many such teachers become eager to collaborate with myself and with other teaching colleagues on related activities. Others have begun to rethink their classroom environments to create unique and adaptable learning spaces that provide opportunities for making and creating, moving away from an instruction-as-consumption-of-knowledge paradigm. Makerspaces offer new horizons and opportunities for us across the 21st-century learning landscape that will help to propel our students into a better and brighter future for themselves.

CHAPTER
11

School Leaders

*"Creativity and innovation is the product of intentional
leadership."*

—Disney Institute

Creating a culture of innovation will only work fully and
effectively if the initiative is able to claim real and ongoing
commitment from the top of the organization (Robinson, 2011).
The Maker Movement in schools can only be successful with the
help of school leaders who not only encourage valuable innovation in and by our students but who also recognize that teachers
need the freedom to be innovative as well. By invoking the spirit
of the Maker Movement itself, digital-age school leaders can emulate a "get it done" mindset to encourage a learning environment
of digital age challenge, excellence, and collaboration (Martinez &
Stager, 2014). Key to the success of my makerspace was an admin-
istration that, in a sense, stepped out of the way, did not raise

unnecessary barriers to change, and actively nurtured a culture in my school that allowed for creativity and innovation to occur. My library needed a new vision and my principal at the time, Eric Sheninger, gave me complete autonomy over my budget as well as real ongoing support to transform the space.

The Maker Movement has served as an impetus for school leaders to critically reflect on the learning spaces and environments that embody their school. Do they meet the needs of learners today? Do they foster and inspire creativity, provide flexible opportunities to learn, and address unique and specific interests? Are they harbingers of what students will expect in today's world and in the world they face in the future (Sheninger, 2014)? School leaders have to understand that a maker culture needs innovative spaces that support it. This means allowing their teachers the flexibility to create different, adaptable, and unique learning environments that work for kids. Great leadership in this context, just as in any context really, is not about micro-managing or trying to determine every nuance of school policy and practice, but about establishing an atmosphere of trust, permitted risk taking, and professional and personal responsibility being given to staff to do their very best at all times. In schools that want real and deep-seated pedagogical change, the leadership will seek to work with teachers, with students, and with the wider school community to transform learning spaces and environments so that they truly support the kinds of instructional changes desired.

In light of the Maker Movement, school leaders need to understand that they do not have to have all the ideas—they simply cannot anyway. They need to acknowledge the breadth of talent and knowledge of their staff and to consider sincerely the inherent value that their staff will bring to the process of change, given the encouragement and the trust to do so. The role of a creative leader is not to have all the ideas; it is to create a culture where everyone can have ideas and feel that they are genuinely valued (Robinson, 2011). Decision making should be decentralized to the greatest extent possible, and school leaders should trust their teachers and give up some control. Risk taking and failure should not be discouraged. In fact, in order to encourage innovation, school leaders should make it safe to take risks. Doing this will allow teachers to think creatively and outside the proverbial box. "Fail fast, fail often" is a common mantra among Makers and the subcultures it overlaps—design thinkers, "innovators," etc. The idea is that you want to iterate, to improve, to fix things, that failure is how you learn (Eason, 2014). Effective school leaders cultivate an environment where there is freedom to learn from failure in order to grow and become better. The greatest risk to innovation will be from a leadership that takes no risks, that brooks no "failure," and that tries to retain the maximum amount of control possible over all the workings of a school.

The support, trust, and encouragement of the school leadership are self-evidently critical to the success or otherwise of any attempts to build a working maker culture in your school. But in many ways, equally important is the technical leadership that can be brought to bear on establishing the makerspace by your school or district tech team. The relationship you build with the tech team—in many schools that will be a team of one!—will play a big part in determining how quickly and effectively you will get your makerspace up and running and then operating successfully over time. In New Milford, I was lucky to have a great District Technology Coordinator in Ron Watson, who not only showed great willingness to get involved in the planning, testing, procurement, and installation of equipment and resources for the makerspace, but also very quickly became a champion for it, both in the school and beyond—the latter most evident in his enthusiastic tweeting about the makerspace on many occasions. Building a strong relationship with your tech team, as well as with other key stakeholders in the school community such as your school's custodians/caretakers, admin staff, and others, will prove invaluable to the long-term success of your makerspace.

And these relationships also point up the importance of your own leadership role in setting up and running your makerspace. By taking on the task, you will soon find yourself doing a million and one things to get everyone on board; to build enthusiasm for the project; to resist those who might not see a makerspace as a bona fide use of the school library, or who might simply dismiss it all as students playing with toys; and to continually think up great ideas and little sparks of imagination to inspire students and your colleagues to make full use of the makerspace.

Ultimately, when it comes to the makerspaces themselves, school leaders should be open to the idea of making for the sake of making. A makerspace can have activities associated to the Common Core and even can be assessed; however, making doesn't always have to be—indeed, I would argue, *must* not always be—tied to traditional assessment. Many teachers and school leaders alike often fear how students can be appropriately assessed in maker environments. This fear has been established as a result of a reliance on transitional methods of assessment as the only valid means to measure learning. Rather than focusing on just formal assessment, consideration should be given toward traditional focusing on acknowledging the granular skills students gain in this space and providing a way for them to get credit for, celebrate, and validate that learning.

Making all of this work requires leadership: your own leadership of the makerspace project; your school and district leadership that offers a trusting, relatively autonomous space within which you and your colleagues and your students can take risks; the technical leadership of your school or district tech team; and of course, the willingness of the whole school to permit the learners themselves to take on the leadership of their own learning needs.

References

Balsamo, A. M. (2011). *Designing culture: The technological imagination at work*. Durham, NC: Duke University Press.

Canino-Fluit, A. (2014, June). School library makerspaces: Making it up as I go. *Teacher Librarian*. Retrieved from http://www.highbeam.com/doc/1G1-373680327.html

Carman, P. (2009). *Skeleton Creek*. New York, NY: Scholastic Press.

Coffield, F. (2000). *The necessity of informal learning*. Bristol, CT: Policy Press.

Common Core State Standards Initiative. (2014). *English Language Arts Standards » Anchor Standards » College and Career Readiness Anchor Standards for Reading*. Retrieved from http://www.corestandards.org/ELA-Literacy/CCRA/R/

Eason, H. (2014, June 10). Integrating empathy into the maker movement [Web log post]. Retrieved from http://thehillarylp.com/blog/2014/6/10/integrating-empathy-into-the-maker-movement

Gustafson, B. (2014, July 16). Makerspaces [Online forum comment]. Retrieved from https://community.theeducatorcollaborative.com/groups/library-media-specialists/forum/topic/makerspaces/

Hickman, L. (2009). Dewey: Pragmatic technology and community life. In S. Rosenthal, C. Hausman, & D. Anderson (Eds.), *Classical American pragmatism: Its contemporary vitality* (p. 101). Chicago: University of Illinois Press.

Higher Education Funding Council for England. (2006). *Designing spaces for effective learning* [PDF]. Retrieved from http://webarchive.nationalarchives.gov.uk/20140702233839/http://www.jisc.ac.uk/media/documents/publications/learningspaces.pdf

Hlubinka, M., DeRose, T., Dougherty, D., Wilkenson, K., & Petrich, M. (2012). MakerClub playbook [PDF]. Maker Media. Retrieved from http://youngmakers.org/resources/playbook/

Hlubinka, M., Dougherty, D., Thomas, P., Chang, S., Hoefer, S., Alexander, I., & McGuire, D. (2013). Makerspace playbook [PDF]. Maker Media. Retrieved from http://spaces.makerspace.com/

Hodgson, K. (2010, August 29). My 25-word story collection on Prezi [Web log post]. Retrieved from http://dogtrax.edublogs.org/2010/08/29/my-25-word-story-collection-on-prezi/

Hole-in-the-Wall. (2013). Retrieved from www.hole-in-the-wall.com

Illich, I. (1971). *Deschooling society*. New York, NY: Harper & Row.

Illich, I. (1973). *Tools for conviviality*. New York, NY: Harper & Row.

Institute of Play. (2014). *The real work of a 21st century education*. Retrieved from http://www.instituteofplay.org/about/

Jackson, S. (2014, September 8). Back to school with the Maker Movement [Web log post]. Retrieved from http://www.fredrogerscenter.org/blog/back-to-school-with-the-maker-movement/

Jenkins, H., Clinton, K., Purushotma, R., Robison, A., & Weigel, M. (2006). Confronting the challenges of participatory culture: Media education for the 21st century (The MacArthur Foundation). Retrieved from http://www.macfound.org/media/article_pdfs/JENKINS_WHITE_PAPER.PDF

Jenlink, P. M. (1995). *Systemic change: Touchstones for the future school*. Palatine, IL: IRI/Skylight Training and Pub.

Johnson, D. (2010). Changed but still critical: Brick and mortar school libraries in the digital age. InterED. Retrieved from http://www.doug-johnson.com/dougwri/changed-but-still-critical-bricks-and-mortar-libraries-in-th.html

Kolk, M. (2011, September 9). Tinkering and creativity—a natural partnership [Web log post]. Retrieved from http://web.tech4learning.com/blog-0/bid/66669/Tinkering-and-creativity-a-natural-partnership

List of tool-lending libraries. (n.d.). In *Wikipedia*. Retrieved December 15, 2014, from http://en.wikipedia.org/wiki/List_of_tool-lending_libraries

Lowery, G. (2014, June 18). Made in Space to showcase Space Manufacturing at White House Maker Faire [Web log post]. Retrieved from http://www.madeinspace.us/space-showcase-space-manufacturing-white-house-maker-faire

Maker culture. (n.d.). In *Wikipedia*. Retrieved October 9, 2014, from http://en.wikipedia.org/w/index.php?title=Maker_culture&oldid=628480935

Maker Faire. (n.d.). In *Wikipedia*. Retrieved December 16, 2014, from http://en.wikipedia.org/wiki/Maker_Faire

Maker Faire: A Bit of History. (2013, January 18). *Maker Faire*. Retrieved December 16, 2014, from http://makerfaire.com/makerfairehistory/

Makerspace@Lakewood City Schools. (n.d.). Retrieved from http://www.makerspacelcs.com/

Martinez, S., & Stager, G. (2013). How the Maker Movement is transforming education [Web log post]. Retrieved from http://www.weareteachers

.com/hot-topics/special-reports/how-the-maker-movement-is-trans forming-education

Martinez, S., & Stager, G. (2014, July). *The Maker Movement: A learning revolution.* Retrieved from http://www.iste.org/explore/articleDetail? articleid=106

Matus, M. (2014, July 28). Makerspaces: A revolution in sustainable production [Web log post]. Retrieved from http://www.custommade.com/ blog/makerspaces/

Next Generation Learning Challenges Grant Recipients. (2014). Retrieved from http://nextgenlearning.org/grantee/lakewood-city-school-district

Parker, J. (2014, September 23). Re-imagined learning spaces for media centers [Web log post]. Retrieved from http://www.personalize learning.com/2014/09/re-imagined-learning-spaces-for-media.html

Partnership for 21st Century Skills. (n.d.). *Framework for 21st century learning.* Retrieved from http://www.p21.org/our-work/p21-framework

Pullinger, K. (Author), & Harper, I. (Producer). (2005). *Inanimate Alice.* Retrieved from http://www.inanimatealice.com

Quaglia, R. J., Fox, K., & Corso, M. (2010, November). Got opportunity? *Educational Leadership, 98*(3). Retrieved from http://www.ascd.org/ publications/educational-leadership/nov10/vol68/num03/Got-Opportunity%C2%A2.aspx

Rix, K. (2014). Meet the makers. *Scholastic Administrator.* Retrieved from http://www.scholastic.com/browse/article.jsp?id=3758299

Robinson, K. (2011). *Out of our minds: Learning to be creative.* Oxford, UK: Capstone.

Robinson, K., & Aronica, L. (2009). *The element: How finding your passion changes everything.* New York, NY: Viking.

Root-Bernstein, R. S., & Root-Bernstein, M. (1999). *Sparks of genius: The thirteen thinking tools of the world's most creative people.* Boston, MA: Houghton Mifflin.

Schwelm, M. (2014, February 13). Makerspaces, learning & libraries [Web log post]. Retrieved from http://www.jpmakers.com/makerspaces-learning-libraries/

Science, Technology, Engineering and Math: Education for Global Leadership. (n.d.). Retrieved from http://www.ed.gov/stem

The 70 Percent Solution. (2005, December 1). Retrieved December 12, 2014, from http://money.cnn.com/magazines/business2/business2_ archive/2005/12/01/8364616/

Sharples, M., McAndrew, P., Weller, M., Ferguson, R., FitzGerald, E., Hirst, T., & Gaved, M. (2013). *Innovating pedagogy 2013: Open University innovation report 2.* Retrieved from http://www.open.ac.uk/personal pages/mike.sharples/Reports/Innovating_Pedagogy_report_2013.pdf

Sheninger, E. C. (2014). *Digital leadership: Changing paradigms for changing times.* Thousand Oaks, CA: Corwin.

Stager, G. (2014, June 23). Playground poem [Web log post]. Retrieved from http://stager.tv/blog/?m=201406

The Tinkering Studio. (n.d.). Retrieved December 15, 2014, from http://tinkering.exploratorium.edu/

Trilling, B., & Fadel, C. (2009). *21st century skills: Learning for life in our times.* San Francisco, CA: Jossey-Bass.

United States Department of Education. (n.d.). *Science, technology, engineering and math: Education for global leadership.* Retrieved December 16, 2014, from http://www.ed.gov/sites/default/files/stem-overview.pdf

Wiggins, G. P., & McTighe, J. (2007). *Schooling by design mission, action, and achievement.* Alexandria, VA: Association for Supervision and Curriculum Development.

A SAGE Company

Corwin is committed to improving education for all learners by publishing books and other professional development resources for those serving the field of PreK–12 education. By providing practical, hands-on materials, Corwin continues to carry out the promise of its motto: **"Helping Educators Do Their Work Better."**